This book belongs to

Sarah Epstein is a designer, illustrator and award-winning author happily creating in her colourful studio in Melbourne, Australia. She has a Bachelor of Design and has worked in creative industries for over 30 years. Visit **sarahepsteinstudio.com** to find out more about Sarah's artwork and books, and also find Sarah online here:

○ **sarahepsteinstudio**   ♪ **sarahepsteinart**

▶ **sarahepsteinstudio**

Published by Fourteen Press, 2024
Melbourne, Australia

Text and illustrations copyright © Sarah Epstein, 2024

Cover and internal design: Sarah Epstein

ISBN 978 1 76370 352 0 (hardcover)
ISBN 978 1 76370 351 3 (paperback)
ISBN 978 1 76370 350 6 (ebook)

To find more of Sarah Epstein's artwork, visit:
sarahepsteinstudio.com

Sarah Epstein Studio

Birds in my Australian Back Yard

Sarah Epstein

14 PRESS

Australia is home to a variety of fascinating birds, brightening the landscape with their vivid colours and boundless energy. Whether gliding through the skies or exploring the ground, these birds are full of surprises.

They're not just eye-catching, they are also essential to the environment, spreading seeds, pollinating flowers and keeping insect populations under control.

With birdcalls ranging from laughter to whistles to musical notes, and even the ability to mimic sounds, these vibrant characters make Australia a magical place for bird lovers.

Have you spotted any of these feathered friends in your own back yard?

Sulphur-crested Cockatoo

Cacatua galerita

Size: 48-55cm.

Eats: Berries, seeds, nuts and roots.

Voice: Extremely raucous screech ending in a slightly upwards inflection.

Habitat: Varied vegetation types and timbered habitats.

Feathery facts:

• Feeds on the ground.

• When feeding, one or more members of the group watches for danger from a nearby perch.

• Chicks remain with the parents all year round.

• Family groups will stay together indefinitely.

Superb Fairy-wren

Malurus cyaneus

Size: 11-14cm.

Eats: Mainly insects, including grasshoppers, ants and larvae. Also small seeds and fruits.

Voice: Thin zizzing musical trills. Alarm calls are heard as a louder, repeated 'chit'.

Habitat: Open forest, swamps, coastal areas, rainforest and gardens.

Feathery facts:

• Forages mostly on the ground.

• Nests are built less than one metre from the ground, most often in thick grass or shrubs.

• Plumage of the male is blue and black with a blue-black throat and a white breast and belly, whereas the adult female is mostly brown with a white throat, breast and belly.

Rainbow Lorikeet

Trichoglossus haematodus

Size: 30cm.

Eats: Nectar and pollen, fruits, seeds and some insects.

Voice: Strong 'screet, screet' and noisy chattering.

Habitat: Rainforest, open forest, woodland, heath (scrubland), gardens and urban parks.

Feathery facts:

• Sociable, noisy and acrobatic.

• Often seen in loud and fast-moving flocks, or in communal roosts at dusk.

• Acclimatised well to urbanisation and commonly encountered in well-treed suburbs.

• Eggs are laid on chewed, decayed wood, usually in a hollow limb of a eucalypt tree.

Australian Magpie

Cracticus (Gymnorhina) tibicen

Size: 36-44cm.

Eats: Insects and their larvae.

Voice: Flute-like carolling, often performed as a duet or by groups. Harsh shrieks for long distance calls and when they feel threatened.

Habitat: Open forest, farms and urban land.

Feathery facts:

• Lifespan of 25 years.

• Very territorial. During the breeding season some will become aggressive towards intruders, including humans, that venture too close to their nest sites.

• Females lay three to five blue or green, brown-blotched eggs, that are incubated for 20 days.

Crimson Rosella

Platycercus elegans

Size: 35-38cm.

Eats: Seeds of eucalypts, grasses and shrubs, as well as insects and some tree blossoms.

Voice: Brassy 'kweek-kweek' in flight and a bell-like whistle when perched.

Habitat: Moist forests, farmland, parks. Some also live in sub-coastal mountains and woodlands.

Feathery facts:

• Forages in trees, bushes and on the ground.

• Active during the day, and at night they roost on high tree branches.

• Nest is a tree hollow, located high in a tree, and lined with wood shavings and dust.

Scarlet Honeyeater

Myzomela sanguinolenta

Size: 9-11cm.

Eats: Nectar of flowers, and sometimes fruit and insects.

Voice: Males give a tinkling song from a prominent perch. Also 'chiew, chiew' contact calls are made by both sexes.

Habitat: Mangroves, open eucalypt forests and woodlands, especially those near wetlands.

Feathery facts:

• Lives a solitary life but occasionally seen in pairs or flocks.

• Distinctive red colouring earns them the nickname 'bloodbird'.

• Small cup-shaped nests suspended from horizontal branches or in a fork, constructed from fine bark and grass bound with spider web.

Laughing Kookaburra

Dacelo novaeguineae

Size: 40-48cm.

Eats: Insects, worms and crustaceans. Small snakes, mammals, frogs and birds may also be eaten.

Voice: Raucous 'koo-koo-koo-kaa-kaa-kaa' chorus, as well as a shorter 'kooaa' used as warning.

Habitat: Open forest and woodland.

Feathery facts:

• They are not really laughing when they make their familiar call. The cackle is a territorial call to warn other birds to stay away.

• Prey is seized by pouncing from a suitable perch, and small prey is eaten whole.

• Believed to pair for life.

Willie Wagtail

Rhipidura leucophrys

Size: 19-22cm.

Eats: Insects such as beetles, larvae as well as flies, spiders, wasps, bees, ants and grasshoppers.

Voice: Sustained 'chittit-chittit-chittit' alarm around predators, melodious whistle-type call, and singing at night during breeding season.

Habitat: Everywhere except very wet forest.

Feathery facts:

• Wags tail from side to side while foraging, zig-zagging in short runs along the ground to flush insects from ground cover.

• Aggressive and territorial, often harassing much larger birds such as Kookaburras.

• Nests are constructed using fine dry soft grasses and other plant material, woven together in a neat cup shape using spider webbing.

Galah

Eolophus roseicapillus

Size: 35cm.

Eats: Seeds, mostly from the ground. Also seeds of grasses and crops, making them agricultural pests in some areas.

Voice: High-pitched 'chri-chri' screech.

Habitat: Woodland, open shrubland, grassland and parks.

Feathery facts:

• Congregates in huge noisy flocks to roost together at night.

• Forms permanent pairs, though they will take a new partner if the other one dies.

• Creates nests in tree hollows or similar, lined with leaves.

• Can breed with other members of the cockatoo family, including the Sulphur-crested Cockatoo.

Gouldian Finch

Erythrura gouldiae

Size: 14cm.

Eats: Ripe or half-ripe grass seeds as well as insects.

Voice: A high-pitched whistling 'ssitt'.

Habitat: Open woodland and grassland.

Feathery facts:

- Move in flocks to more coastal areas and return inland to breed when the rainy season arrives.

- The only grassfinch that nests exclusively in tree hollows or holes in termite mounds.

- Seldom found far from water, and needs to drink several times a day.

- Bright colouration has led to them being a target for the illegal bird trade.

Yellow-tailed Black-Cockatoo

Calyptorhynchus funereus

Size: 56-65cm.

Eats: Wood-boring larvae, and seeds of native and introduced trees and ground plants.

Voice: Wailing 'kee-aaah' and a staccato 'growl'.

Habitat: Open forest, pines and farms.

Feathery facts:

• One of five species of Black-Cockatoo in Australia.

• Feeds in small to large noisy flocks.

• Both sexes construct the nest, which is a large tree hollow lined with wood chips.

• Usually only one chick survives, staying in the care of its parents for about six months.

Australian King-Parrot

Alisterus scapularis

Size: 40-45cm.

Eats: Seeds and fruit.

Voice: Loud 'carrak-carrak' in flight, and a far-carrying, shrill piping whistle by the male.

Habitat: Moist, tall forest and nearby farmland. Also orchards, parks and gardens in autumn/winter.

Feathery facts:

• Normally encountered in pairs or family groups.

• Lay their eggs on a bed of decayed wood-dust at the bottom of a deep hollow in the trunk of a tree.

• Increasing in abundance in well-treed suburbs. In urban areas they feed at artificial feeding stations and fruiting trees.

New Holland Honeyeater

Phylidonyris novaehollandiae

Size: 16-20cm.

Eats: Flower nectar, fruits, insects and spiders.

Voice: Strong, high-pitched 'chik' and a fainter 'pseet', as well as some chattering notes.

Habitat: Heath (scrubland), woodland with dense shrub layer, and gardens, mainly where grevilleas and banksias are found.

Feathery facts:

- Their tongues can protrude well beyond the end of their beaks to probe for nectar in deep flowers.

- May feed alone but normally gather in quite large groups.

- Both sexes feed the chicks. A pair of adults may raise two or three broods in a year.

www.ingramcontent.com/pod-product-compliance
Lightning Source LLC
Chambersburg PA
CBHW041242020426
42333CB00003B/58